People Skills

How To Become Comfortable To Talk To Anyone And Make Friends Without Being Awkward

By

John Guzman

Table of Contents

Introduction 5

Chapter 1: The Right Mindset To Make Friends 8

    All Kinds Of Worries 8

    The Confident Mindset 13

    Be Less Self-Absorbed 14

    Be Willing To Venture Out Of Your Comfort Zone 16

    Always Be Willing To Talk First 17

    Always Look For Things In Common 18

Chapter 2: Developing The Right Mindset To Make Friends 20

    How To Build Confidence 20

    How To Tackle Anxiety/Shyness 24

    How To Stay Relaxed In Every Situation 28

    How To Naturally Become More Extroverted 31

Chapter 3: Finding Friends 41

    The Right Places To Find Friends 41

Using Social Media/The Internet To Find Friends 45
How To Make Friends Spontaneously 50
Making Friends In School/University 52
Making Friends In A New City 53
Be Discerning 55

Chapter 4: Starting Conversations..... 60

First Contact – Body Language 60
Different Ways Of Starting A Conversation 63
Don't Create Differences 76
Ending The Conversation With A Great Impression 83
Conversation Hacks 90
Recognizing And Using Different Conversation Styles 97
The Five Conversation Styles 99
Different Cultures, Personalities, And People 105
How To Have More Substantial Conversations .. 107

Chapter 5: What To Do After A Conversation? 111

Set A Point Of Future Contact 111
Using The Mere Exposure Effect 113

Ask Them For Help 115
Send A Memorable Message 115
Send Them An Offer..117
Make Someone Feel Good..117

Chapter 6: Problems With Making Friends.. 119

When Your Life Circumstances Interfere With Your Social Life...120
When People Don't Seem Interested In Starting Friendships With You 124
When You Don't Have Friends At All 128

Conclusion 131

References 135

Disclaimer....................................... 141

Introduction

You try to talk to someone and your voice gets stuck in your throat. You walk away, humiliated and frustrated at your lack of social skills. If you learned some real people skills, you would have conversations more easily, find friends left and right, and even stumble upon greater opportunities in life.

I should know all about this. As a shy introvert unable to talk to people, I was missing out on life quite a lot. I realized that I needed to improve my people skills if I wanted to work in customer service, which was my first job. Through months of practice and studying research about social skills, I finally found the formula that enabled me to become comfortable with people. Now I'm not shy at all and I have many great friends, a huge business network, and luck with getting dates.

If you want to be like me, then you are reading the right book. You can change. The benefits of having social skills are countless. Think landing jobs at the first interview, making friends with one conversation, and avoiding awkwardness at parties. Think asking your crush out and getting favors. Think confidence and happiness in your own skin. Your whole future will open right at your feet.

The truth is, you can't survive without social skills because humans are a social species. You must learn how to interact. This book will show you how to do just that. From starting conversations to getting over your fears, this book will help you develop the skills that will get you far in life.

I promise that by the end of this book, you will be a new person. Your relationships and self-confidence will both improve. But you must do your part – you must read this book and actually use the information contained!

If you don't do this now, you can expect a lifetime of regrets, shyness, and feeling passed over for every promotion. Leadership opportunities, great friendships, and successful business will all be unavailable. You must start building these vital skills immediately.

So, what are you waiting for? Start on your journey to become a social people person!

Chapter 1: The Right Mindset To Make Friends

Like everything in life, mind is over matter. Your mindset drives how you act and how you present yourself to others [1]. Therefore, you must have a certain mindset to make friends.

All Kinds Of Worries

What is wrong with your mindset now? The answer requires some introspection. Most people can't make friends due to some kind of worry that chokes them up. They give off a sense of nervousness and fear, which others find off-putting. They may even be so nervous that they don't even try to talk to people at all. The result is social awkwardness driven by fear. Obviously, the solution is getting rid of the fear, but first you must identify what that fear is.

I Am Too Old

Or I am too fat, I am too ugly, I am too stupid. There are a million different ways to express the same fear: that you are not good enough for other people. You find something you don't like about yourself and magnify it into an issue that seems completely insurmountable. You assume others won't like you because of whatever this insecurity is.

Chances are, other people don't like you, but it has nothing to do with your insecurity; it has to do with the fact that you make it very clear you are not confident in your own skin. People can sense that, and they run away because they desire confidence [1].

Your insecurities and flaws are usually more pronounced to you than to others [2]. You notice what is wrong with you and make it a whole part of your identity. Other people might notice your flaws, but they are not going to refuse to be friends with you because of them. They want to see confidence.

In a study, participants were asked to rate their fatness. Most people rated themselves as at least two-thirds wider than they really were [2]. This was most pronounced in women, but it was true of men as well. The point of this study was to prove that our flaws are smaller in the eyes of others. We tend to magnify our flaws, including our weight, and we look better to others than we do to ourselves.

The key to getting over this is learning to accept and love yourself. It also involves realizing that other people don't judge you as harshly as you judge yourself. Others tend to be too wrapped up in their own problems to magnify your flaws. The exception may be someone working in a modeling agency or

Anxiety Because Of Failure

Maybe in the past you tried to make friends and they rebuffed you. Now you are scared to try again. The truth is that some people are unkind or going through bad things in life, so they don't respond well to your attempts to make friends. You can't let that prevent you from trying again.

Many people use something called generalizing, or globalizing [3]. This is where they base their judgments of others on one person or one experience. You are globalizing everyone you could make friends with based on the one person or group of people who did not respond well to your friendliness. That prevents you from meeting the people out there who might embrace you as a friend.

Consider if you were bullied in school and now you are not very social. The thing is, people tend to grow up after school and leave behind that juvenile hostility. In the real world, you can meet adults who will not reject you as your high school peers did. So, don't overgeneralize and assume everyone is like your high school bullies.

Shyness

Some people suffer from shyness. Some even go on to develop social anxiety. While these two things are not the same, they are similar in that they induce irrational fear of speaking to others and having social interactions. These issues may be caused by a past trauma, an abusive childhood, or simply a chemical imbalance in the brain.

If you find yourself taking a different route home just to avoid talking to your neighbor, dropping eye contact, and shunning social engagement, you may suffer from social anxiety. This is a mental disorder that can be treated with cognitive behavioral therapy, social anxiety coping groups, and social skills practice sessions. It may even be treated by medication. It's time to seek help to improve your life with social skills and normal social interactions.

The Confident Mindset

Confidence is attractive, to the point where people seek it in others [1]. If you are confident, then you let others know that nothing is wrong. Then they can feel at ease. The entire group is content, and socializing can take place unimpeded. This stems from our evolutionary roots, when we needed to feel at peace from threats like lions and wolves. While our world may be safer in some ways now, that instinct lingers on, permeating our social atmosphere.

In fact, confidence is so attractive that people will make decisions based on the confidence that they detect in another [1]. Basically, being confident makes you someone that others look up to and turn to for guidance. You make people feel safe as if you are their leader when you project confidence. Not projecting confidence leads to discouraging people from making decisions [1].

From this, you can gather that having a confident

mindset is the right mindset for making friends.

Be Less Self-Absorbed

To make friends, your mindset must embrace social interaction and be interested in others. Only then do you show others that you like them and want to hang out. This makes them like you, and thus friendships are cemented.

Imagine the most self-centered person in your office or social life. She or he talks on and on, and never asks other people what they are feeling or thinking. She/he never remembers names and doesn't talk about other people or ask how their days are going. No one really likes him/her; they tolerate him/her with eye rolls. Well, this is a prime example of a person with few friends because of her high level of self-absorption.

It's time to put yourself aside and quit talking about yourself incessantly. You certainly can mention things about yourself, but you need to turn your focus outward. This is especially difficult for introverts but it's crucial. Talk to people and ask them about themselves. That will create far more friendships than talking about yourself.

This means that you need to remember names and birthdays. You need to ask someone, "How was your day?" Ask about a person's hobbies. And really listen when they answer you. Stop thinking about yourself and think of others, and you will get great results.

"That lady who never shuts up in the adjacent cubicle never talks about anybody else and she has friends," you might say. The thing is, she doesn't really. She injects herself into conversations, so it seems like she has people to talk to. But really, everyone ignores her. She has no true friends.

Be Willing To Venture Out Of Your Comfort Zone

Your comfort zone is a safe place where you hide. In it, you don't try new things or meet new people. That's great except that it ensures your life never changes in any way. Only when you venture out of this safe space and start experimenting with what life has to offer you will you begin to make friends.

In your little bubble, you don't cross paths with many new people. You also don't have much to relate on with new people. But when you try something new, you put yourself out there, crossing paths and developing things to talk about. Plus, you seem more interesting and more confident because you are willing to explore the world.

Many people claim that making friends as an adult is hard. It's only hard because adults tend to settle into a rut. They keep the friends they have and don't bother to make new ones; they have their hobbies and their routines and don't vary much. Thus, they don't meet and interact with new people, and they don't make new friends. However, you can change that by being willing to put yourself out there.

Always Be Willing To Talk First

People often won't come to you and talk first. The reason is explained before: they are set in their ways. Why talk to someone new? Some of them may be just as shy as you. Only when you speak first do you make people notice you and respond.

Therefore, you must change your mindset to one that enables you to speak first. You must be willing and ready to start new conversations with new people. Chat with the cashier at the convenience store, the barista at your favorite coffeehouse, the bartender making your drink. Say hi to your co-worker and ask him how his weekend trip went. Call your old friends first to catch up.

Being the first to speak puts you in the unique position to control and steer the interaction. You can make someone notice you, respond to you, and realize who you are. You just opened a pathway to a potential friendship.

Always Look For Things In Common

People like that which is similar to them [4]. They seek things in common because it makes them feel comfortable and safe by inducing similar neural activity [4]. When a person finds something in common with you, he or she automatically likes you more and has more to talk about with you. The bond strengthens based purely on that single commonality. Similarities may range from having the same favorite basketball team or sharing a mutual friend.

So, when you are meeting a new person, you must have the mindset to create bonds over similarities, not divisions over differences. Instead of looking for ways to disagree about politics or differ in hobbies, look for ways to share a bond. Find something you two share, even if it isn't much.

Chapter 2: Developing The Right Mindset To Make Friends

Now that you know the right mindset, you may still wonder how to go about building it. After all, just reading about a mindset doesn't cause you to acquire it. It takes some work to bring your mindset up to standards as one that relates to others and makes friends easily.

How To Build Confidence

Your insecurities are a part of you. You can't just ignore them. Instead, try to negate them.

"I'm fat," your mind says. Tell your mind, "OK, I weigh a little bit. But I still have a pretty face and I love my curves! I'm also a really great person."

"I'm old," you think. Tell yourself, "I have a lot more wisdom under my belt and I have had a lot of life experience. I'm full of cool stories."

Find things that make you feel not good enough. Then negate them with positives. There is always something good about you to outweigh the negative. This is not to say that you have nothing negative about you – we all do. But these negatives can't be at the forefront of your mind, stopping you from making friends, because you are guaranteed to have good traits too.

Also, try to see how little these negative things really matter. Is a true friend going to care overly much that you have a weight problem or are a bit older than he or she is? Are other people as obsessed about your flaws as you are, or are they more likely to ignore them because they are focused on their own flaws? The correct answer is the latter. People don't notice or care about your flaws as much as you do [2].

Make a list of the good things you do each day. Make another list of the good things about yourself. These two lists can help you see that you are not all bad. There are plenty of things to love about yourself.

Start to work on your self-talk. This is how you talk to yourself. What does your inner monologue sound like? If it has a lot of "You always do this," "You will just fail again," "You are so [insert negative adjective]," or "You are not good enough, I hate you!", then it's time for a change. Focus on chasing those self-hating thoughts with more positive ones. "I can do it!" "I'm a good person." "I think I will do well at this."

Approach things from a more solution-oriented mindset as well. Should you fail at something, think, "What can I learn from this to make the results better next time?" If you think you can't do something, think how you can learn how to do it right. If you have a flaw you hate, think how you can improve it and take those steps.

Another tip is to set up a series of little goals that you

can achieve. As you achieve them, your belief in yourself grows. The next thing you know, you are tackling much bigger and more significant goals. Start just with what you can do today to prevent yourself from feeling overwhelmed. Then, move on to grander goals.

Finally, stop comparing yourself to some standard set by someone else or yourself. Your body is not made to look like a Victoria Secret Angel's; that's OK. You are not supposed to have everything figured out by any age; you can screw up now and then. People tend to impose comparisons on you, or you tend to impose them on yourself. You look to others for models of how to be and then feel awful when you fall short. It's time to stop those thoughts as you start thinking them. Remind yourself that you are a unique person with a unique set of life circumstances, so of course you will be different. Comparisons are not accurate and not helpful.

As you do these things, you start to love yourself. That makes you more confident. Confidence comes from within, as you start to see the good in yourself and embrace it without letting the bad in yourself ruin your entire self-image. You start to believe that you can do things and you are worthy of better than what you have been getting in the past.

How To Tackle Anxiety/Shyness

If the idea of meeting new people makes your knees knock together, you are far from alone. A lot of people have social anxiety or shyness – an estimated 15 million adults in the United States, as a matter of fact [5].

Social anxiety can be addressed with cognitive behavioral therapy, which you can perform on yourself. Get a CBT workbook on Amazon and begin to address the thinking that makes you so socially anxious. This helps you rewire your brain so that you talk and act differently, favoring helpful and positive thoughts over negative, harmful ones.

If social anxiety incapacitates you to the point that you can't leave the house or make eye contact with anyone, then you need some help. Social anxiety can be debilitating but you can mitigate that. Therapy and medications usually work well to restore your quality of life. Even if you feel that you are not incapacitated by social anxiety, getting help is not a bad thing.

Shyness can be overcome simply with practice. You can start by practicing in a mirror. When you feel more confident with what to say, start to practice at places like bars or coffee shops where you don't know anyone. Make small talk with the barista, for instance. With practice, your confidence grows, and you start to navigate social interactions more confidently and securely [6].

You should also make yourself more vulnerable. By

admitting to having emotions, you can find points to relate to people on [4]. If a woman is telling you that her dog died, you can empathize and create more of a connection. You can even mention how your dog died once too. This is just an example of how being vulnerable can help you shed your shyness and start to actually relate to people. Shyness tends to make you freeze up and try to act perfect, which in turn makes you seem unnatural. Being vulnerable helps you relax and bond with people better.

Being vulnerable also entails being your authentic self. You can't focus on being perfect or you will blow it because no one is perfect. You also can't focus on your flaws, or you will become self-conscious and shy as a result. Instead, you must think, "I am who I am. Take me or leave me." This powerful attitude comes across as confidence because it is the very essence of confidence. Other people will see it and like you more. If you act self-consciously, then you draw attention to your flaws and put other people off. Avoid being self-conscious or apologizing for yourself; just be you, no apologies.

Another tip is to use powerful, confident body language, AKA power posing [7]. Power posing involves having an open body language. You don't cross your arms or legs, shrink into a chair, or turn away from people. Rather, you face them squarely, with your arms and legs open. You keep your head high and your neck and back straight. You walk with purpose, swinging your arms wide. When on a couch or chair, relax into it and place your arms over the back of it. These little things tell people that you are one confident person and you already know how that helps you gain friends. By using a power pose at all times, you make others respect you more, which leads to positive social interactions. As a result, you forget your shyness as people come to you.

Finally, stop focusing on the things that make you feel afraid or insecure. Focus instead on other people. Listen to them and think of things to say. This keeps your mind off its anxiety and helps you stay present in the conversation. That will do you wonders.

The more you talk and the more you get into a conversation, the more relaxed and confident you become. That also makes you more vulnerable – more authentic. Shyness will trickle away with practice [6].

How To Stay Relaxed In Every Situation

If social situations make you nervous, you can't be expected to just relax and be at ease. But with some work, you can get there. Being relaxed tells other people that you are OK, so they are OK too; it is that crucial sense of safety that confidence gives others [1].

The first key to relaxation starts with breath. You use breath calm your body and tell yourself that everything is OK. Your brain responds by reducing the adrenalin that makes you jittery and full of dread. You breathe in through your nose and then out through your mouth.

Keep it rhythmic. Start breathing well before a social situation and then breathe through it and you will enjoy much more relaxation. Actors will use breathing before an audition or performance; singers use vocal exercises to achieve this.

Another key is to stop the huge amount of anxious thinking shooting through your brain. You can do this by being mindful of the present situation. Stay aware of what others are saying and what they look like. When your thoughts start to wander toward "How do people here think of me?" and "What am I doing?" draw them back by focusing on someone's face or words. Being mindful is essential to letting go of worries and feeling more at ease.

Mindfulness is basically mental control. You can identify and control your thinking. You will find that a daily mindfulness meditation helps you get this control. The simplest exercise involves staring at a spot on the wall with full concentration. You can't think about anything else. If you do, you gently acknowledge the thought and then bring your attention back to the spot on the wall. With time, this becomes habit that enables you to control your thinking and stay present and relaxed.

Some people use alcohol or drugs to relax. While these things certainly work, the problem is that they make you a fake person in any social situation. People get to know you for the person you are when under the influence of something. Then, if they meet you sober, they are surprised by the change and even put off. Plus, you can make a bad impression if you are always drinking or taking drugs, and you may not be able to use these substances you come to rely on in certain situations that require social skills, such as a job interview. It is far better to let people see the real you. That is the only one to build true connections that go deeper than the effects of drugs and alcohol.

How To Naturally Become More Extroverted

One of the biggest misconceptions about introversion is that introverts are shy. This is not true at all. Introverts are simply people who get energy from within, not from others. Therefore, they are great at working alone or being alone, and may even need alone time to recharge. However, they are not shy by default. Many introverts display extroverted characteristics, being talkative, confident, and outgoing in social situations. Many of them like having friends as well.

The average introvert is a private person. He likes talking about others more than himself. He prefers one-on-one conversations to talking to whole groups of people. Nevertheless, he needs and can perform in social situations. With proper social skills, you can't even tell he's introverted, unless you get to know him well and find out he needs his private time to recharge.

Introverts are not shy, but shy people are introverted.

That's the key difference. If you are shy, becoming an extrovert will not help you, nor is it possible. But you can learn social skills that make you a very social introvert. Remain an introvert and be comfortable with who you are, and you will succeed socially. The more comfortable and accepting you are of your introverted characteristics, the better you will do in social situations anyway. Your confidence will bloom from accepting who you really are.

Extroverts are people who draw energy from others. They must work on teams, have friends, and talk to others to be happy. The stereotype is that they are always the life of the party, but in fact, shy extroverts do exist. Shy extroverts crave the attention of others and even need it to thrive, yet they can't build bonds out of fear. They have a unique set of problems that they must overcome by learning proper social skills.

If you are a shy person, it does not matter if you are introverted or extroverted. Shyness is an issue in and of itself. Overcoming shyness has nothing to do with changing your personality type from introvert to extrovert. However, if you want to become more like an extroverted person, it is possible. Observingin and adopting the characteristics of a social extrovert provides the guidelines for being a social and comfortable person.

The Meyer-Briggs personality test uses a series of questions to find your personality type. Out of sixteen types, half are introverted, and half are extroverted. Your personality is fairly static; it will not change with time, nor can you make it change [8]. You are better off accepting your personality type and working with it to be social, as opposed to trying to change it, which is impossible. That is the key to naturally becoming more extroverted in your behavior. If you are an introvert and you embrace that, you can get over social anxiety and shyness, and become a very social and comfortable introvert that other people like. Instead of changing who you are or being fake, you can just learn to talk to people comfortably, relax in social situations, and have a good time without feeling anxious. Get over fear of social situations and get over insecurities to become a social magnet.

Introverts are more than capable of being social and having great social lives. They just need some alone time and they tend to think better alone. Taking some time to recharge and make decisions is important for you to do if you are introverted. On the other hand, extroverts who are shy can grow confident in who they are and learn some social skills, with absolutely no issues barring them from becoming extroverted in behavior.

The main key to becoming more extroverted in your behavior entails talking more. You just have to talk, that's it. Tell jokes, tell stories, ask people about how they are and what they feel about the current affairs. Making conversation puts you out there and makes people relate to you. You don't hang back in a corner, waiting to be spoken to; you speak to people as if they are already your friends.

Always smile and talk first. That draws people to you. Offer your hand for a firm handshake and introduce yourself first. These small things make people notice you and relate to you. Hanging back in shyness will cause you to be invisible.

You want to speak first often, as well. Say there's an impromptu meeting. Being the first to open your mouth and lead the meeting makes everyone take note of who you are and what you have to say. This is something extroverts do – speaking without permission or fear. They just let out what they are thinking without inhibitions. They enable people to identify with their thoughts and create bonds, and they make themselves heard.

Also, get out more. Introverts like to stay where they are familiar and comfortable, thus causing them to miss out on new social possibilities. Therefore, you must go to new places, such as new bars, new churches, or new book clubs. Try new activities that take you out of your element. This is all part of the mindset you must adopt to make people like you more because you get to meet new people and develop new topics for conversation if you explore the world around you.

If you can't get out a lot, then at least delve deep into a hobby. That will help you meet others while giving you lots to talk about. No matter what the hobby, you are likely to find others who share it.

Say yes more than no. If someone invites you out, there is your chance to make new friends. Accept invitations and initiate yourself in new social situations. Even just catching up with old friends can help you relearn social skills and confidence.

Try to go out with someone, instead of alone. People are more drawn to you when you are with other people.

This relates to the Principle of Likability proposed by Dr. Robert Cialdini [9]. The Principle of Likability states that people tend to like things that others like. So, if you appear in public with other friends, you are instantly more likable.

Take this example: You go to the bar to pick up chicks. No one talks to you. You seem like some creepy weird guy who is sleazing the girls at the bar. Then you take a buddy the next time and girls feel more comfortable talking to you. You have probably encountered this before and it's true of life: Having friends makes everything better and people talk to you when you are not alone.

Another key is to keep in touch with people. Once you meet someone, find out how to stay in contact, either through social media or in person. Exchanging contact information is a great way to start friendships and it is a more extroverted thing to do. The more you meet someone and talk to them, the more they like you. The result is a friendship born of mere exposure [10]. The mere exposure effect means that people like something the more they see it, so exposing people to your face is a good way to get them to like you. Most introverts don't want to bother people and don't reach out enough, so be persistent in reminding people that you exist.

Another extroverted thing to do is to talk to people as if they are already your friends. You don't need to get overly personal, asking questions and sharing things that are not appropriate. But speak to someone affectionately, ask them how they are, and keep track of things like birthdays. Remember details. These activities make people like you more and feel as if a friendship is already formed. Avoid being overly formal or bringing up how little you know each other. Instead, say things like, "How nice seeing you guys! Let's have a good time like last time."

Be like people who are extroverts. Watch how they

stand in the center of groups or the center of the room and talk to everyone. Avoid finding a comfortable corner to hole up in, where you appear like a wallflower that no one wants to talk to. Don't just stick to one-on-one conversations all the time or stick to one friend. Try to talk to everyone. Introverts do better with one-on-one conversations, so you can make the rounds and meet everyone, having various one-on-one conversations. Don't just hold one and call it a night, or you just limited how many people you got to meet.

If you are an introvert, doing these things can drain you completely. You must avoid letting yourself get drained or you can become discouraged and give up on this personal work. The best bet is taking some time to yourself to recharge. Go to your house or favorite place to be alone and let yourself recharge on your own energy. That's what introverts are best at, being alone. You need some time on your own to clear your mind, organize your thoughts, and regain the energy to keep being extroverted. Go back out when you're ready. Try to make a habit of going out more. Over time, being extroverted will come naturally because your brain is used to it and no longer has to expend as much energy doing it.

Chapter 3: Finding Friends

You can learn social skills all day long, but what good do they do if you can't use them? Finding friends is easy enough in school, when you are surrounded by people you share at least a few things in common with such as age. But as an adult or in a new city, it can get a little more challenging to find friends. Finding them is still possible, however.

The Right Places To Find Friends

The right place to find friends depends on who you are and what you are looking for. A good starting place has to do with your particular interests and hobbies. You probably won't find a lot of friends in a church if you are an atheist. Hanging out with people who are diametrically opposed to your personality is not ideal, though you can certainly try it and see if you're surprised. Sometimes, trying new things exposes you to elements of your personality that you never knew existed. However, you usually know who you are, so stick to that and you will make friends who are like you. It is easier that way.

It is a safer bet finding something that you enjoy doing. Then you will naturally be at ease and other people will relate to you more. Look at a list of things you like to do or have always wanted to try and then find similar activities in your area. As long as you harbor interest in things, you will be more likely to project to others that you are having a good time, and that radiant positivity will draw people to you. There is nothing like a genuine smile to make people like you.

You should also look at things that you have always wanted to try but never have. Doing new things will expose you to new people and new opportunities. Always wanted to go sky diving? Do it! There is no reason to stay in your shell. Exiting your shell can be scary, but enlightening. You might never run into someone special or find out who you really are if you never try anything that scares you a little bit. Most shy people find extroverted activities, like improv, giving speeches, or going to mixers and business networking socials, very challenging. Since you are trying to become more social, it may be your best bet to visit some of these things and expand your horizons.

However, some activities are naturally more introverted. A community garden may be a place to make friends, but you're more likely to spend your time there alone. Try to pick out activities where you will meet new people, such as classes or workshops or even teams. If you are a crafter, go for a knitting club. If you are athletic, play an intramural sport. Do something that lets you meet others, rather than go off and be alone. The idea here is not to spend more time alone but to have opportunities to strike up conversations with strangers. The more people in an activity, the more likely you will find some new friends at it.

Try activities that you already have friends in. Having a friend can set you more at ease and help you seem more appealing to others [9]. Then you can make friends through your friend. Since you don't want to be a nuisance and cling to your one friend, you will feel pressure to expand your horizons and meet others. Take advantage of that. Be careful not to pigeonhole yourself with one group of people; try to talk to everyone present at the event or activity. That way, you can make new friends and be comfortable should your friend not arrive one time.

Social clubs are another good place to meet people. If you are a veteran, like volunteering, or want to play a role in your community, check out clubs for your interests. You might find a home at the VFW, Eagles, or Moose lodges. You might enjoy taking part in a Women's Club or the Boys and Girls Club.

Volunteering is a great place to meet people with similar interests and causes. Try volunteering at a place where you feel passionate about its cause. The shelter for animals, Habitat for Humanity for housing the homeless, the DA office for working with crime victims, and other such charities are out there. Often you can visit your local city hall for a list of local volunteer opportunities.

If you are religious, you can find a wealth of friends and support at a church, mosque, synagogue, temple, or prayer group. Trying new churches or temples can help you unlock your true spiritual calling. You will meet many people who are eager to get to know you and guide you on your spiritual journey.

Using Social Media/The Internet To Find Friends

In the Internet age, there is no better way to make connections. Social media allows you to meet people in a superficial way so that you can form a friendship. Then, when you meet, it's less awkward because you have already gotten to know each other a little bit and have things to talk about.

Chat rooms are a great place to meet people. You can find chat rooms for anything that you are interested in. Facebook groups and LinkedIn groups also let you find people with similarities to you and can help you grow your social and professional spheres. Finally, check out websites for organizations that you may be interested in joining.

Online dating is a nice way to meet new people, despite its bad reputation. Get to know each other for a while. Then go on a date in a public place and let someone know where you are going to stay safe. Dating sites that vet their members usually charge fees, but they are worth it.

Try Meetup to find local groups and activities. There are some meetups for every kind of hobby. Some meetups are just social clubs, where you can meet over coffee. The best thing about Meetup is that you can check out profiles of members of each meetup before going, to ascertain if you would fit in with this crowd. Meetup lets you try new things and meet new people. If you have never been to a floristry club, but you love arranging flowers, try it out. If you have never been bungee jumping, you can probably find a group that does that on here. If you want to learn a dance, you can probably find a club that does that dance and is eager to teach you.

If you have a specific interest, there is probably an online community for it. Online communities range from the ordinary to the bizarre, so find your niche. Even if you just like sharing funny cat photos, you will find people who love that too online.

Offering to help people learn English or learning a new language can help you network with people you never knew existed. There are a plethora of free language practice sites. You can tutor English or learn another language by receiving tutoring. This connects you with people from all over the world. Most of them are quite friendly.

Couchsurfing is a cool way to meet new people. It is an international network with chat and events. You can use it to find people in new areas to hang out with or even stay with for free. You can be a host and let people passing through your city stay in your home if you feel comfortable. If you don't, you can just meet people to hang out with or go to big Couchsurfing events. There is no obligation to ever meet in person or to host anyone.

The first key to social media networking involves building a winning profile. A lot of people lie on social media, but this makes it awkward when you try to meet people in person. Upload an accurate photo, fill out as much information as you can, and be truthful. Include photos of things you care about, like your artwork or your pets. Make this profile an extension of the real you. Try to find places to mention the coolest things about you, such as that time you went to Europe after college or your interest in model trains. The more you put on there, the more you prove to people that you are someone they would like to meet. Avoid mentioning overly personal or negative things, as this can deter new friends.

Be friendly and send people messages introducing yourself. A simple "Hi! I saw your profile and I think we could be friends" is sufficient. Stay on top of messages and reply to people in a timely manner. Try chatting about things you have in common and ask them lots of questions about what they are interested in.

Your online friends could be local people that you meet with in person. Or they could be long-distance friends. Those friendships can be just as fulfilling because you have someone to talk to. You can get to know people quite well online and see sides of them that they would never show in person. Some people claim that online friendships are not real, but if you get satisfaction from them, then that is the whole point.

How To Make Friends Spontaneously

To make friends spontaneously, you need to reach out to the people around you and put yourself in new situations. Reach out to neighbors, co-workers, and other people you have not previously talked to and try to find things in common to do. Go to new meet-ups or new places and talk to people.

To start a friendship, you want to find as much in common as possible. This increases your chances of having a common ground to start from. If you both like fly fishing, hey, there's a great place to start. You can invite this person to go fly fishing with you. That is just an example of one of the million things you can do to make friends.

In public places, comment on similarities with people. At a book shop, you can say, "I read that book. I highly recommend it." At a coffee shop, compliment someone's taste in beverage. Comment on someone's clothes with a nice compliment or comment on the music playing. Using environmental factors can help you find points of commonality with others. Stay observant to find things to talk about.

You can also listen to what someone is saying. If he or she is not locked in a private conversation, you are probably welcome to jump in with a comment that could kick off a connection. For instance, if you overhear someone telling the bartender about a local business closing, you can chime in with, "I heard that too. It's really sad! I used to go there all the time." That just ignited a new conversation.

Also, watch for clues. If someone says, "I have never been to that museum," propose that you go together. If a person wants to try a new type of food, say, "Let's have a quest to find that cuisine!"

Center conversations around things you know. If someone is into books, talk about the books you know and ask them about the books they like. If someone wants to talk about current events, be sure to chime in. Politics and religion are often argument starters, so you may want to avoid such topics at first.

The more interesting things you come up with, the more likable you will be. If you find things to do that you both enjoy, your friendship can grow and become solidified. Try to make it action-based at first and then the more personal conversational aspect of the friendship will grow from there.

Making Friends In School/University

Schools and universities are full of opportunities to make friends. It is best to start in your classes and offer to help people study or propose study groups. Engage in conversation with your fellow students and find out who they are and what they like. If you talk to them enough, you might find things you want to do together, or you might get invited to a party. Don't be afraid to extend invitations to people to hang out.

Another great thing to do is to become involved in clubs and activities. Find something that interests you. not only do extracurriculars look great on your transcripts and resumes, but they help you broaden your horizons and meet new people you may have never met before.

Go to games and student meetings. Go to the library and smile at people. If there is a party, go. All these things make it easy to tap into the diverse population at your school.

Making Friends In A New City

Moving to a new city can make finding friends difficult. Without knowing anyone, you can't make the Principle of Likability work in your favor. Therefore, you must break the ice somehow.

The best way is, again, activities. You may also benefit from doing things at work, such as conventions, picnics, and office parties. When your co-workers go out for drinks, tag along. Say yes to as many opportunities as you can.

Many cities have social media groups for new people. You can make a post, "I'm new here and I want to know what I can do to make friends." Doing this will help you connect with other new people and by doing so, you can meet friends.

The other activities mentioned before work well, too. Find a hobby, get involved in a church, take part in a community endeavor, and/or volunteer. Take classes or join clubs. All these things can help you meet new people.

Often, it just takes one friend to get you out of your bubble. One friend can introduce you to a wealth of new people. Therefore, you want to work on finding that one person who is interested in being friends with you. Talking to lots of people and doing activities can open you up to a wealth of people, but just one person is often enough to get out there.

Feel free to ask new people you meet to show you the city. They can introduce you to new friends while showing you what a good time is in the new location. Don't be afraid to ask questions and ask to be introduced to new people.

Be Discerning

Most people who are shy are eager to make new friends. Therefore, they let their guards down and stumble into some very bad friendships. Predatory people can see your eagerness and take it as vulnerability. They will prey on you.

When meeting new people, it is essential to be discerning. You want to watch others. Consider this an audition, where you are not only making an impression, but you are deciding if other people are right for you.

There are many red flags to watch out for. If you spot one of them, don't pursue a friendship with that person. Dangerous people can pose as friends and then reveal their true colors later, but they often slip up and let you see one or two red flags immediately.

The first red flag involves people who are two-faced. She might be nice to you, but observe how she talks about other people in the room. If she smiles at someone and then turns around and speaks ill of him or her, that's a sign that she will speak ill of you too.

Avoid gossips. These people will do anything to get you to tell them secrets. Then they will tell everyone. They are not safe or trustworthy people. They will also twist things you say or make up stories. If someone is gossiping to you, don't feel like you're on the inside. Understand this person is a chronic gossip who will gossip about you when you leave the room.

People who tell even white lies are suspicious. They are likely pathological liars who embellish the truth to serve their needs. Once you catch someone in a lie, you should be wary. Everyone lies now and then, so you can forgive someone for a small lie, but you should proceed with caution. Chances are, this person will keep bending the truth to suit his or her needs.

People who must put you or others down generally have low self-esteem and can't celebrate the victories of others. These are the people who tell you, "Don't get a big head, dear" or "You got a promotion? There was one summer where I got five promotions! Back to back!" They either cut you down or find a way to one-up you. You will always find that you can't please these people and they will never cheer you on or encourage you.

Watch out for people who make you feel like you can tell them all. Often these people are manipulators who are adept at getting information out of you. The best bet is to be very private and reserved with your personal information until you get to know someone very well.

Also, watch out for people who many enemies. These people may play the victim and have great stories for why everyone hates them. But the truth is usually that someone with so many enemies deserves them. Listen to someone's reputation and proceed with caution. Chances are, people are right when they say "Watch out for that person!"

If someone constantly makes you feel bad, that's another red flag of a manipulative person. Say you're eating a potato salad and the person says, "I wish I could eat potato salad! You're so lucky that you don't have to watch your figure." You instantly feel bad about eating the salad. That's a sign that this person doesn't want anyone else to have what he or she can't have.

The friend who asks for a favor may not be a bad person. But watch out for future favors. You may find that this person is taking advantage of you. Be sure to set boundaries and put limits on how much you're willing to do for a person without getting anything back.

Obeying these warning signs helps you determine who is really your friend and who isn't. You can avoid or at least limit contact with those who appear to be toxic or unsafe friends. Always take your time to get to know someone.

Chapter 4: Starting Conversations

When meeting new people, all it takes one conversation to help form a friendship. A conversation enables you both to see if you should pursue the friendship or not. You obviously wouldn't want to continue a friendship with someone who talks about all her deep personal problems on the first meeting or someone who admits to enjoying torturing animals. A rude or cold person is also a deterrent. But if you both find things in common and like each other's personalities, a conversation is a gateway to a more profound connection.

First Contact – Body Language

Before you even open your mouth, your body language says a bunch of things that the other person can interpret loud and clear. From there, the conversation really hinges on your body language. The first impression you make in a conversation is always a silent one. Since at least 56% of your language is comprised of body language, 38% tone of voice, and the rest what you say, you need to be mindful of your body language to send the right message [11].

First, you want to focus on your facial expression. Facial expressions are universal, so people from all cultures will understand what your smile, frown, or grimace means. Smiling tends to get the most positive reaction from people; in other words, a smile can make someone want to talk to you [12]. For some reason, smiling also tends to make people judge you as more intelligent [12].

Some people "resting bitch face syndrome." This is not a real medical syndrome, but rather an anecdotal phenomenon. Basically, when your face is relaxed or in a neutral expression, it looks like you're angry. Resting bitch face syndrome can make people feel put off because they perceive you as angry and unapproachable when you're a really nice person. In social situations, plaster a smile on your face and don't let your face relax into a scowl.

Next, consider eye contact. Making eye contact shows a level of interest and comfort that can open a conversation [13]. But holding it too intensely for too long can be perceived as threatening. Try to avoid making too much eye contact; break eye contact every twenty seconds or so. However, looking away more than that can make you seem shifty or nervous, which is a deterrent [13]. Make eye contact first and smile and you have created a connection that may lead to a conversation.

Watch your stance. Being fidgety, slouched, or tense can convey that you are uncomfortable [13]. Being relaxed and holding your head high says that you are confident and ready to have social interactions [13]. Avoid crossing your arms and legs, as these things can seem like you are closing yourself off or being threatening [13]. Also avoid sticking your hands in your pockets, as this too can be taken as a sign that you have something to hide [13].

Different Ways Of Starting A Conversation

There are two main ways to start a conversation: risky and safe.

The safe way is easy enough. You make a comment about the weather or something pertaining to the conversation you want to start. You make an innocuous comment about the music, someone's clothes, or something else. These conversation starters won't offend anyone, but they can bore people. They are a great way to start when you are practicing.

Risky is a little more entertaining. This is where you catch someone by surprise. They include blatantly political comments, challenging someone to a game, teasing someone, a pick-up line, or even a joke that may be offensive. People may not respond – but if they do, they will be more interested in you than otherwise.

To start a conversation the risky way, you want to size up your conversation partner first. If you hear him making ribald jokes, for instance, you know he won't mind if you make one of your own. If she is wearing an anti-president shirt, you know how your views may match or clash with hers. Consider how the person looks, acts, and talks to determine how to best approach him or her.

Breaking The Ice

To break the ice, you might need to be the first to speak. People won't notice you or go out of their ways to talk to you in most cases. It falls on you to start the conversation.

If you are standing next to someone and an awkward silence has ensued, it's time to break the ice. Say something to make a conversation happen. You can start practicing this on strangers in the elevator or with work colleagues to get comfortable with it. Remember, practice makes perfect!

A great ice breaker pertains to what is going on around you. Mention the game playing at a sports bar, someone's clothes, or someone's choice in appetizer. Making observations allows the other person to identify with you because you are both observing the same thing.

Another great one is to comment on current events. Most people are familiar with what is going on right now in the world. If they say they don't know what you're talking about, you can fill them in. They may ask questions and a conversation is born.

Yet another way to go about breaking the ice involves making some sort of joke. Most people like jokes. And if you make a funny one, you just intrigued that person. It may turn into an exchange of jokes.

Asking a person lots of questions about who they are and what they do is another way to break the ice. People prefer talking about themselves. When they meet someone who seems curious, they are eager to share. Look at a person's stance and clothes or office décor for clues about what they may be interested in. A lot of people leave clues about their personality everywhere to be found.

Finally, you can break the ice by mentioning something interesting about yourself. "I was in the army" could be a way to bond with another person who appears to be in the military or ex-military. Or "I used to work there" can start a conversation with someone who works at a certain place. Try to find something in common that you can gather about a person and then find what you can say to create that conversational bond.

Once you break the ice, the person has a choice to respond or not to respond. People who don't respond probably just don't feel like talking. Don't take it too personally. People who do may respond minimally, so you must keep the conversation going.

Remember And Say Names

When you meet a person, be sure to catch his or her name. Repeating this person's name multiple names can create a connection and cement a friendship [14]. In fact, experiment with this the next time a waiter serves you at a restaurant. Note his or her name and then use it whenever you ask for something. Notice how the server smiles and responds more genially. At the end of the meal, smile and thank your server and repeat his or her name. You will get excellent service this way.

Why does this happen? The brain activates a certain way when it hears its own name. There is considerably more activity within the middle frontal cortex, middle and superior temporal cortex, and cuneus when one's name is heard compared to the names of others [14].

When you do this in conversation, you make a person feel stimulated. You also excite the person's attention, creating a sort of attraction that is not sexual in nature. This attraction can make a person feel good around you, which causes him or her to want to keep talking to you. The person feels validated and heard if you use his or her name.

So, learn someone's name. Then repeat it often throughout the conversation. "Hey, Roger, so how is your job going?" "That's great, Roger. What is it that you do there?" Don't make it seem unnatural, just repeat the name a few times each conversation.

This goes on to repeating other facts and details you remember about someone. It can make people flood with dopamine and feel happy when you remember his or her birthday, for instance. Try to learn and remember as much as you can. Writing these things down in an address book can help you memorize them.

In future conversations, repeat things you learned about the person. "I remember you saying that you don't like Italian, Roger. Do you really want to go to that restaurant?" is an example of how you can sneak little details you remember into conversation in a natural way. Roger will be flattered that you bothered to remember his culinary preferences and a friendship is more likely to flower.

Continuing The Conversation

A lot of courses teach you how to start conversations. You may be a master at it by now. But what these courses fail to mention is how to keep it going. A conversation can quickly become dead in the water if you don't know how to keep it going.

Find Relevant Topics

When talking to someone, you want to find a relevant topic that you can both enjoy. A common interest is an excellent place to start. If you both love the same music, you can spend hours conversing about bands and songs that you both know. You can even show each other new songs. Finding that topic that takes up the bulk of your conversation is essentially finding the conversational sweet spot.

But it can take a few tries to find that sweet spot. You might have to bring up several topics. The way to find the sweet spot is to ask questions that start with who, what, where, when, and why. As you ask these, you can get more information from a person and learn what he or she may want to talk about.

You also need to be mindful of the other person's cues. If a person starts looking at exits, fidgeting, or checking their watch or phone a lot, you know that he or she is bored. It's time to switch topics. Bring up something new or ask a new question to renew the person's interest.

It's also OK to switch topics if you feel bored or uncomfortable. Except for some rude people who are totally blind to conversational cues, most people can tell when you're getting bored and restless. They may drop the conversation there. You can keep it going by proposing a new topic during the next lull in conversation.

Rapid conversational topic switches can throw someone off and cut off their thought process for a moment. Therefore, you want to stay more or less on topic. Just propose a new subtopic.

Topics Everyone Loves

Most people will be stimulated by the following topics and will have lots to say.

Family is one way to start and keep a conversation going. You might notice a picture of someone's child on his or her desk, so ask about the child. You will likely get some details that you can elaborate on. If you have a child too, you can find things to say to relate to the other person on. Or you might mention that you have no kids, but you want them one day. Family doesn't have to be about kids, either, as you can talk about any family members you find relevant to the conversation.

When you see someone, you haven't visited in a while, ask about how his or her family is doing. Listen and respond positively. Offer sympathy when the person mentions something sad or negative. Then mention your own family and things you two have in common.

Sports are another good topic. Not everyone loves sports, so if someone says, "I don't like sports," you know that's not the conversational sweet spot. But if someone does love sports, a conversation about it is likely to ensue. Ask them what their team is and mention how they played in the last game. Talk about your team and what you played in high school.

Music can get a lot of people talking. Ask someone what their taste in music is and compare. You can show each other new bands and songs if you have similar taste. Even if you have different taste, you can compare and contrast your favorite genres.

Culture is often a great conversation starter. Without appearing xenophobic, you can mention, "I haven't met too many [insert culture here]. Could you tell me more about it?" Asking people questions about their homelands, cuisine, and religion can really broaden your own knowledge and cultural sensitivity. Most people love talking about their cultures.

The same goes for travel. People love talking about where they are from or where they have traveled. You should mention if you have been to the area they are talking about or haven't been there to determine where the conversation goes. You can talk about your experiences there or you can learn all about it from the person.

Work is a boring topic for some people, but everyone will tell you what they do and describe their jobs if you ask. Then, you can talk about your job. Commiserate on the things you hate, such as long hours, and chat about the things you do like. Focus on the positive more than the negative to avoid being a drag.

If someone has a pet, that's always a good source of conversation. Ask them about their pets and talk about your own. Even show them pictures. You will likely get some pictures in exchange. People love their pets and will enjoy talking about them.

If some catastrophe, severe weather, or major political event has happened, that can be a conversation piece. Mention, "Did you hear about that tornado?" While this is more of an ice breaker than anything, you can keep the conversation going by sharing a story about how you survived a tornado as a kid. Or mention how the weather is just getting worse every year. Current events can lead to a range of subtopics as you can touch on many things in the conversation. You can also learn some new things if the person you are talking to has some news or rich gossip you haven't heard.

Some topics are just banal. The weather is a good example. No one likes to spend hours talking about what a nice day it is. You can use the weather as an ice breaker, but then find something somewhat related to talk about to open a conversation. For instance, if you use the band playing at a bar as an ice breaker, you can switch the topic and keep the conversation going by talking about other bands you have heard. Don't just focus on that one band or the conversation can get boring fast.

Be Positive

I am sure you have had the unlucky experience of talking to someone who just complains and brings up negative things the whole time. It is not a fun conversation. You don't want to be that Debbie downer of you can pull the conversation down with you.

Being positive is good for conversation [15]. People tend to respond to positivity better than negativity. Don't start by saying, "I work at [insert company name] and I hate it. My boss is a drag." You should instead make light of it and joke about how you work more than you live, or something to that effect.

Point out the silver lining in every situation. That makes people feel good. Then they want to keep talking.

Don't Create Differences

How familiar does this sound?

Someone asks you, "Do you like fishing?"

"No, I hate being outdoors."

"Oh." The conversation ends there.

In this example, you just created a difference. That just made the conversation grind to a halt. You didn't attempt to find anything in common with the person. You just used negativity to shoot down their attempt at breaking the ice.

Many of us inadvertently create differences. But of course, we want to create similarities to spark similar neural responses that correspond to friendship [4]. That doesn't mean you should be fake and lie that you love fishing when you don't. You should just try a little harder to find something in common.

Back to the example, try this instead:

"Do you like fishing?"

"Not particularly. I'm not an outdoors person really. But I do like the taste of fish!"

The other person will probably laugh and talk about the great taste of some fish he caught last weekend. A conversation is born.

Use Dr. Cialdini's Principle Of Influence

In his book *Influence: The Psychology of Persuasion*, Dr. Robert Cialdini outlines six principles of influence that can make people do what you want [6]. These principles can easily be used to make people like you and keep a conversation going.

The first principle, reciprocity, is where you give someone to get something in return. This is the principle at play when you buy someone a drink at the bar and nine times out of ten, the person will come over to talk to you. Offer someone something small in exchange for conversation, such as offering to buy them a drink or bringing them a plate of food at a party.

The next one, commitment and consistency, is where people like their behavior to match their values. So, if someone cares deeply about something, you want to match that in your conversation. Talking to someone about what they would normally talk about makes them feel consistent and therefore good. It can keep the conversation going.

Social proof is where other people do what you are doing. So, if you wear a suit to a party, other people will wonder if they should have worn such a nice outfit. In conversation, you can make people copy you by starting the conversation on a certain topic.

Being an authority on some topic will make people gravitate to you because people love respecting authority. Using big words correctly and talking knowledgeably about something makes people want to listen. It can spark lots of conversation.

Social proof is where you get people to like you by already having other people like you. Having a friend at your side is a good way to get more people to talk to you. Otherwise, you can make people like you by giving them sincere compliments, smiling, and asking them questions about themselves. You don't have to have a friend at your side to make friends. It just makes things easier because friends can prove to others that you are a likable person.

Scarcity is where people feel that you are in limited supply, so they want to talk to you before someone else does. Being the sharpest looking person in the room, having the most unique things to talk about, and being kind can make clamber all over you. Then others will want to talk to you because you appear to be in short supply.

How To Win Friends And Influence People

Influence is a fantastic book about making people like you, but so is Dale Carnegie's famous *How to Make Friends and Influence People.* Carnegie describes some ways to get people to want to talk to you and to keep conversations going.

The main way Carnegie recommends you keep a conversation going is to be genuinely interested in other people. Instead of thinking about what you are going to say next, relax and focus on what the other person is saying. The other person will be able to see your interest and desire to talk. They will appreciate how you seem laser focused on their words and how you keep asking questions to find out more.

You want to make steady eye contact with breaks every twenty or so seconds. You also want to face the person and lean into him or her [13]. These things convey interest. As he or she talks, nod and offer the occasional affirmation to prove that you are listening.

Ask questions related to what they say to learn more. When you speak, keep it on the same topic.

You should also smile a lot, according to Carnegie [16]. Carnegie understood how important smiling was without even knowing the brain chemistry behind it. Seeming enthusiastic, happy, and positive will keep the conversation going longer than being negative and pessimistic.

Focus on the person's interests and don't let your own crowd out the conversation. Keep talking about what the person wants to talk about. If it is a boring topic, find a way to make it interesting. Let the other person do the majority of the talking to make him feel as if you are truly fascinated.

Finally, make the person feel important. If your conversation partner mentions that he works in the meat packing department at a grocery store, don't downplay his job. Mention how important his job is.

That will flatter him and make him keener on talking longer.

Ending The Conversation With A Great Impression

If you use Carnegie's tips, you should exit the conversation having made a great impression [16]. Simply making the person feel important and listening well makes you seem like an outstanding conversationalist. Nevertheless, there are still other things you can do to make this person walk away thinking, "What a great person! I want to see him/her again."

The first key to keep on top of your appearance. If you stink or have dandruff, you make a bad impression. You tell other people that you don't care about yourself, so how can you possibly care about them? You need to have basic hygiene down and you need to try to smell nice. Dressing in flattering clothes and wearing a flattering hairstyle is also essential. Looking like a dumpster when you have conversations will repel people.

Wearing red can help you make a good impression [17]. In several studies, women rated men wearing red as more attractive. A little red in your attire, such as red lipstick, a red hat, or a red tie, can make others find you more physically attractive. This physical attraction may not be sexual, but it plays a role in making people think that you are a great person. It is also a great job interview hack.

Try to be as tall as possible, which makes you appear more confident and more assertive. People pay attention to taller individuals. Shoes can make you appear taller, as can clothes with vertical stripes. Holding your spine straight can add at least half an inch to your stature. Keeping your arms and legs uncrossed also gives the illusion that you are tall. If you are already a tall person naturally, you're in luck. People have more respect for you naturally. Otherwise, you have to fake it.

The second key is to making a good impression is to avoid being too nosy or personal. You don't want to ask, "So, how often do you shower?" or "Why did you get a divorce?" Most people will disclose things if they want to but asking will put people off. Maintain a polite level of distance in your conversation and don't pry. Good conversation involves asking lots of questions, but those questions are not supposed to be overly personal. It's not a good idea to pry into someone's personal life or ask about painful events. Touching on someone's health may be polite if they mention they saw a doctor or if you know they have an illness, but there are polite limits.

When you sense someone is getting uncomfortable, change the subject. Don't press on any issue that makes the other person avoid eye contact or start to fidget. If someone changes the subject, oblige him or her. You will make a bad impression if you press issues. Learn to drop things once someone asks you to or looks uncomfortable.

Also, don't be confrontational. If someone disagrees with you, don't start arguing. Don't push your opinion on a person. Simply accept your differences and move on in the conversation. Any sign of hostility or overbearing pushiness will make a terrible impression. This is not the time to be right and win. It is the time to make people like you.

Complaining a lot can also make a bad impression. You seem ungrateful if you complain about friends, family, and work. You also seem like a backstabber.

Avoid gossiping. This just makes you seem lower than you really are. Even if others are gossiping, politely excuse yourself from the conversations. Don't repeat what you hear or take part in silly squabbles. Don't offer opinions on arguments or fights that other people are having. None of that is any of your business.

You can be an expert, but don't be a know-it-all. Claiming that you know what you don't makes you look like a fool. Using big words incorrectly does not impress anyone. If you say something and someone proves you wrong, admit it with a smile and say, "Well, I stand corrected!"

There is a time and place for offensive jokes. You can share them with people who you know will enjoy them. Only dip to offensive or vulgar language and jokes if the other person does. For the most part, keep your conversation clean.

Practice good manners. This means holding the door open for people and saying please and thank you. Don't talk about vulgar or overly personal things and don't insult people or the host of an event you are attending. The wisdom "If you have nothing nice to say, don't say anything at all" is critical in making a good impression.

Using a person's name is critical. If you confuse people, be sure to apologize. No one likes hearing anything more than the sound of his or her name as you already know, so be sure to remember it well. Calling a person by the wrong name is very rude but it happens. As long as you apologize and correct yourself, you won't make a bad impression with a simple mistake.

Keep name dropping to a minimum. You can mention who you know to establish things in common with people. Don't use it as a way to impress people, though, or you just look arrogant. Definitely don't claim to know someone better than you do. People tend to do homework and they may find out that you lied.

Truthfulness is always the best way to make a good impression. If you lie to impress people, they may find out. Then they won't talk to you again and they will laugh at you behind your back. It is essential to stay honest. If you don't know something, say you don't know it. If you don't do something, admit it. There is no need to claim that you are someone you are not. You can still make friends being yourself – perhaps more so.

When you make promises, keep them. Follow up on things you said you would. Keep in touch and say hi later on. This proves to people that you are a person of your word. If you can't keep a promise, then don't make it. For instance, if you promise someone you meet that you will investigate a computer issue they are having, be sure to contact them later and offer to look at the computer again. Don't just blow it off or you look like a fickle person.

The final piece of advice is to give people the option to keep in touch. Give them your number or email or social media. Don't ask for theirs. That way, they feel more comfortable reaching out to you. If they don't want to talk again, they won't have to deal with the awkwardness of hearing from you.

Conversation Hacks

Everyone loves hacks. Things that make life easier are excellent, but hard to come up with on your own. Here are some ways to make conversations much easier.

Mirroring

Mirroring is the best conversation hack out there [18]. The simple art of mirroring enables you to create a bond out of thin air simply by mimicking the other person in subtle ways. Besides body language, it is one of the pillars of neurolinguistic programming, where you use body language and speech to trigger the responses you desire in the other person's mind [13].

Mirroring involves mimicking the other person [18]. Studies have shown that people respond really well to this and have more activity in the regions of the brain that correspond to relationships [18]. If someone smiles, you smile; if someone fidgets, you fidget. You watch someone and then carefully copy their movements.

It can get creepy if you are obvious about this. You want to leave a few seconds of a delay between mirroring. You also want to avoid staring at the person hard as you attempt to read their movements. It takes some practice.

Say someone is talking about her dog. She gets a sad face as she mentions that she might have to put him down. Mimic this sad face. She will probably lean into you as she talks more about how she feels, so lean into her. If she lays her hands flat on the table, do the same. Mimic every part of her body language and she will feel more in tune with you, as if you really get her. She will enjoy this and will keep talking to you as a result.

Reflective Listening

Another hack is called reflective listening. Reflective listening is where you repeat back what someone says, confirming that you heard it [19]. You are not thinking about what you want to say or coming up with unsolicited advice; you are simply listening and proving that you heard every word.

It can be very tedious (and weird) to recite an entire paragraph that someone just said. Instead, you want to summarize the information from said paragraph and then reiterate the basics. The person will see that you were listening and will likely give you an affirmation that you heard correctly.

This is where you can practice becoming a bit of a therapist. As a person talks about something, you should nod in agreement, which really encourages them to keep talking. But then you want to reflect what they say. When they agree that you heard right, you can say something like, "That must have made you feel angry." The person will be invited to agree or disagree and thus talk more about his or her feelings.

Emulating a therapist in this way makes people feel good because it proves how invested you are in the conversation. You are listening, you are processing their emotions, and you are a sounding board.

By doing this, you are not inputting your own advice or opinions. This is a bad conversational habit that many people take part in. You are technically blocking communication by doing it. Instead, you want to be a sounding board. It makes the other person think solely about his or her problem, with no impediments to the conversation [19]. This is certainly refreshing and can lead to a new connection that is both strong and satisfying.

Open-Ended Questions

"Do you like volleyball?" you ask someone.

"No," the other person says.

This is an example of a close-ended question, one that can be answered with a yes or no. The conversation can basically die right there if you ask a close-ended question. Close-ended questions don't invite a person to partake in a discussion with you or disclose more information.

It is far better to ask open-ended questions, which require a person to think and deliver an answer beyond yes or no. Take the above example. "What sports are you into?" is a better question because it makes a person think and talk about the sports he or she likes.

When picking open-ended questions, focus on ones about the other person. That way you can invite them to talk about their lives and interests. People love talking about themselves and will prefer to talk about their lives instead of anything else.

Ask For Advice Or Help Of Some Kind

Another conversational hack is to make the other person feel useful. You can do this by appealing to their knowledge and expertise by asking for advice, help, or an explanation. People love proving their authority, so they will gladly share what they know to help you out.

It doesn't have to be a big favor. It can just be something small like, "I know you're in securities and acquisitions. What can you tell me about this stock?" Find what the person knows a lot about based on what they do or talk about and then ask for advice or information.

Also, if someone mentions something that you know nothing about, feel free to say, "Tell me more," or "Can you explain that better?" That keeps the conversation going and educates you while showing that you are an interested listener.

Favors

Asking for favors can be helpful, too [9]. Known as the foot in the door technique, asking for a small favor can open a person up to doing more favors for you. Ask for something small and see how it leads to a friendship. You might ask someone to hold your coat, buy you a beer because you're out of cash, or something else tiny and unimposing. Later, you can give and ask more favors.

You can also do a favor for someone. This acts on reciprocity, where a person feels indebted to you and must return the favor [9]. Buy a friend a coffee the first time you hang out and he will likely buy you something down the road. Creating a give and take of favors is a good way to form a mutually beneficial friendship, as long as no one is taking advantage of the other.

Recognizing And Using Different Conversation Styles

Each person has a different conversation style. If you can communicate with someone on his or her preferred style, or find a person with your style, then you are more likely to communicate well without any misunderstandings. Most misunderstandings are simply things lost in translation between conversation styles. They can inhibit communication and make a friendship impossible to move forward, however, since communication and conversation are essential between human beings.

Nlp Sensory Modal Systems

A sensory modal system refers to how someone views the world around him and then communicates it to others [13]. Following the same sensory modal system of another person can help you understand each other better. The systems are based on the five basic senses: auditory, visual, tactile, taste, and smell.

Most people are visual. This means that they will talk about how things look and they will focus on colors and presentation. They tend to learn better from videos or visual presentations. When they speak, they say things like "Do you see what I mean?" or "Do you picture this like I do?"

When talking to these people, use more visual terms. Recognize the visual terms in their speech and match them. "Yes, I see this. But do you see what I'm saying?" If you match them on visual terms, then you will make more sense and they will feel more validated in what they are saying.

An auditory person talks more about what something sounds like or how something will sound. They use lots of terms relating to sound and they are audiophiles. They learn best by listening. They can often listen to something and remember it clearly. You will recognize this system by the way they say, "That sounds great!" and "How does that sound?" and "Do you hear what

I'm saying?"

The other senses follow the same vein. Tactile people learn by hands-on and touching and talk about how things feel. Taste and smell systems are exceedingly rare but you will also be able to recognize them because that's all the person refers to.

Some people combine different sensory modal systems. If you hear someone combine two or more, then you can probably use whatever system is easiest for you. This person is a great communicator who employs all of his or her senses.

The Five Conversation Styles

Conversation styles also relate to how a person gets his point across. The main styles are assertive, aggressive, passive-aggressive, submissive, and manipulative [20]. People will generally use the same style in every conversation, but you may notice changes when they are addressing certain people. For instance, a person who is usually aggressive to his co-workers may become submissive in the boss's presence, out of deference to the boss.

- **Assertive** communication is generally considered the best because it is confident without hurting others [20]. Assertive people state their boundaries and goals but try to work with others to find a common interest. They make their own choices and take responsibility for them. They keep their body language open and relaxed, speak on an even keel, and have a normal volume and tone of voice. You will hear them say please and thank you.

- **Aggressive** is the opposite. These people often have low self-esteem, so they try to bully others and gain control. They are the ones seen standing in an intimidating way, yelling at people, or overpowering people with their voices. They are often rude and may insult others. They tend to stand too close to people and make eye contact for too long in order to gain dominance. These are the people who must get their way and win, no matter what.

- **Passive-aggressive** communicators are also rude, but not dominant. They tend to be sarcastic and devious, using jokes or snide remarks to hurt others and get their way. They can also be sulky or arrogant, depending on how others respond to them. They speak sweetly while their words are cruel. They stand in an asymmetrical way, such as with a hip cocked out, to show that they are not happy with how things are. Often, when someone leaves the room, they will start speaking badly about that person.

- **Submissive** people don't stand up for themselves. They avoid eye contact and keep to the corners. They stand with their bodies tense, their feet together, and their eyes down. They play the victim and say sorry too much. When they need to stand up for themselves, they usually can't. They let other people make decisions and have the floor when speaking.

- **Manipulative** people use emotions to manipulate others to get their way. They are often high-pitched and give compliments, only to follow them up with insults. An example might be, "What a nice haircut, Marge. It looks so much better than how you usually do your hair." They will sulk, pretend to be sad, or otherwise fake emotions. They are two-faced and bossy. Other people feel guilty around them and don't enjoy their company.

Out of these five styles, the best way to respond to any of them is to be assertive [20]. Keep an even body language and tone of voice. Smile, even if you don't like someone. Stand by your boundaries and say no politely, even to aggressive people who scare you. Don't play games with manipulators, ignore submissive communicators, get into fights with aggressive communicators, or let the sarcasm of passive-aggressive communicators get to you.

Being assertive shows that you have confidence and don't need anyone's approval. You are willing to stand up for yourself, which gains the respect of others. Refusing to play games or buy into someone's sulking can also make them respect you more. Always adopt this conversation style when talking to others for great results.

Question Askers, Open Sharers, And Ambi-Conversationalists

There is a final big conversation style difference: question askers and open sharers. This book has mostly focused on being the question asker. It has encouraged you to ask others questions to learn about them and find grounds to start a conversation on. There is nothing wrong with this, but some people take a drastically different approach.

In the open sharing approach, someone will talk about him- or herself. They volunteer information and answer questions without asking them. They sometimes make their life stories and sharing so interesting that others care and listen. Sometimes, they tend to overdo it, and make people get weary of the conversation. Open sharers tend to make conversations one-sided, all about themselves, which discourages others from participating.

To be a truly great conversationalist, you should be an ambi-conversationalist. This is where you ask questions *and* share information about yourself. You use both approaches to appeal to more people. First practice getting good at asking questions, as that's the easiest way to start conversations. Then practice inserting a bit of information about yourself or opening conversations with comments about your life, hoping that the other person relates and responds. You will find that a mix of the two approaches will actually make people enjoy talking to you more.

Different Cultures, Personalities, And People

Conversation is influenced by a huge variety of factors, which vary from person to person. Personalities, personal beliefs, and cultures can certainly influence how the conversation goes and how the person likes being talked to.

So far, this book has focused on how to make a great impression in the Western world. Being assertive, making good eye contact, firm handshakes, and smiling are all cornerstones of Western communication. They work on most people from American, European, and even some African cultures.

But Asian and Native American cultures are different. In these cultures, people don't like eye contact and consider a firm handshake an invasion of space. You don't ask personal questions and you swap a smile for a neutral facial expression.

Personalities can also be wildly different. You should observe a person to gather his or her personality before attempting to talk to him or her. You might be offensive if you tell a very conservative person a dirty joke, for instance, so watch for that.

The best thing to do is to go by what you know. If a person from a different background becomes offended, say you didn't know and ask, "How would you prefer that I act?" That leads to a conversation in itself. Plus, it makes you appear more culturally sensitive and you can let the other person guide you on how to be toward a certain culture or type of person. Be open to learning and you'll appeal to a broader group of people, which is very helpful in our global society.

The Internet can also help you learn these things. As you can meet a huge demographic of people online, you can learn more about their communication preferences. Talking to lots of cultural groups and religious groups online can help you learn how to speak to them in person. Be sure to ask questions when you feel confused or unsure and stay on neutral topics, or let the other person drive the conversation, until you get more comfortable.

How To Have More Substantial Conversations

A conversation can be boring and dull, focused on sports and the weather. Or it can be fantastic and enlightening, focused on substantial topics. Having more substantial conversations will be more entertaining and lead to more friendships. You don't want to just linger on banal topics; you want to find dynamic things to talk about that you both enjoy.

A substantial conversation can be philosophical, where you delve deep into questions about existence or how life works. But it can also be based on current events and true opinions. It can be about personal things, like how you feel or important stories from your past. It can even involve deep topics like how to fix our government or how to address life problems. A substantial conversation is about more than superficial topics and it touches both of you in profound ways.

Substantial conversations are not always possible. Some people just don't possess the intellect or depth to have such conversations. Some people repress their emotions so well that they don't know how to converse about them and take a conversation beyond the surface-level formalities. Therefore, you cannot expect to have a substantial conversation with everyone.

You can try the waters by posing an intellectual topic or question. See if the other person takes the bait. An intellectual person won't be able to resist discussing such a thing with you. People who can't keep up will get nervous or uncomfortable and not know how to respond. Then you know how to communicate with them and you can lower your expectations.

Also, speak to someone like your friend. This can open the gate to more substantial conversations. You can start by asking a personal question like, "What is your favorite memory?"

Feel free to disclose something about yourself. Something like, "I like stargazing because I gaze up at the stars and think about how they are all probably dead now, and I wonder what the sky really looks like in real time." Something like that will lead the other person to respond substantially. You must become comfortable with a little bit of self-disclosure to speak to someone like a true friend.

Avoid talking about negative subjects. You can have substantial conversations that are all bleak and you walk away depressed. If someone seems to be steering the conversation toward negative subjects, try steering them toward positive or pointing out the bright side.

Otherwise, leave the conversation so you don't get down.

Usually, you will be able to tell if you can have a substantial conversation. It will just feel right, and such topics will come up naturally. You should never feel as if you must force it. Seek out people who like these conversations at events, bookshops, libraries, and other places where intelligent and deep people gather. You may just need one or two conversational partners to get your fix of substantial conversation. Don't expect to have truly meaningful talks at the bar or with party-hearty friends.

Chapter 5: What To Do After A Conversation?

Once a conversation ends, it could be the end of the whole interaction. Or it could be the beginning. The great things about conversations are that they can lead to infinite possibilities. But they can also be fickle and lead to nothing, even if they are wonderful conversations.

When a conversation ends, you can take certain actions to keep it going and make sure it doesn't just die. You want to make sure this person doesn't forget about you. Even if they don't contact you again, you can value the practice you got from this conversation and use it to develop confidence in having future ones that lead to more substantial relationships later.

Set A Point Of Future Contact

The first thing to do is to set up another future meeting. Don't just say good-bye. Say, "I'd love to meet again." Then hand the person your business card, phone number, or social media account. Mention another event coming up or some sort of thing that corresponds to the hobbies that other person loves.

Give it a few days and then call or text or send a request on social media. Make sure that you stay in touch. You may have to do the work initially. This hardly means that a person is not interested in you. It just means that he or she is busy.

Don't text or call constantly, or you will come off as a stalker. You want to be casual and wait a few days.

Better yet, let the person come to you. Give them a really good reason to call you and give them your number. Make sure communication is open. That way, the other person can decide about calling you or not.

Using The Mere Exposure Effect

The mere exposure effect means that someone likes you the more they see you [10]. At least five exposures can make someone like you; fifteen is best [10]. But the mere exposure effect seems to work even better when there is a lapse of time between exposures.

To illustrate this, there was a 1992 study where four women who looked similar attended a lecture [21]. They didn't talk or interact with anyone, they just sat in on the lecture and left afterward. One woman shown up never, one shown up five times, one shown up ten times, and one shown up fifteen times. At the end of the semester, students were asked to rate the attractiveness of all four women in photos laid side by side. Students rated the woman who had shown up to the lecture the most as the most attractive, even though she looked a lot like the other women. This just serves to illustrate how people will like you more the more they see you.

Once you run into someone a few times, you will already have more of a connection. Then, you will start talking more. Be patient and don't expect a friendship to erupt out of one conversation; it often takes many to generate a deeper connection than mere chitchat.

You can set up ways to run into someone several times. For instance, if they attend a business conference, they will probably attend others. You can even ask them if they plan on attending other conferences and then go to those.

It is also easier to make friends with people you have regular contact with for this very reason. Take your work colleagues. You see each other every day and that will lead to more of a connection. It will be easier to invite your colleagues out for drinks than a complete stranger. Attend events outside of work and you will get closer with your co-workers. Or consider attending block parties to get to know your neighbors better, or chat with your neighbors when you pass them or see them at the store.

Ask Them For Help

One way to ensure you see someone again is to ask for their help. If they mention that they design websites, ask them to look at yours and exchange contact info. If they mention that they are expert editors, ask them about how you can get your book edited.

Learn about someone by listening to them. Then find a clever way to compliment them and see them again in one swoop: ask them to use their expertise to help you. That makes it possible to see each other again in the future.

Send A Memorable Message

You met someone. Now you want to make a second impression. The best way to do that is to send a memorable message or email. You might want to reference something that happened when you met, making an inside joke to bond the two of you. Or you might try to refer to something that they told you. Ask a follow-up question. Possibly send a joke or follow up on something you told them about.

For instance, maybe you met someone by bumping into him with a drink and spilling it on him. Email him later asking if he got the stain out and make a joke about your clumsiness.

Or say you told someone that you are breaking up with your significant other. Now you can send a message asking how the person is doing. Add that you broke up. This invites future discussion.

Referring to something that happened or something one of you said is the best to be memorable. You prove you were listening and paying attention, you refresh the person's memory about who you are, and you reaffirm the communication.

Send Them An Offer

Someone happened to mention that her plumbing is bad and she is looking for a new plumber. Do a little research to find a new plumber and send her the information. Letting her know that you were thinking about her and doing her a small favor can help her want to keep talking to you. It shows what a thoughtful person you are, great friend material.

Think of something the person mentioned wanting or needing. Then offer them that thing. This offer will almost guarantee a reply. It also acts on reciprocity and makes the person wants to do something for you [9].

Make Someone Feel Good

People will remember how you made them feel more than anything else. If someone remembers you making them feel good, they will want to feel good again, so they will keep talking to you. Trigger a flood of feel-good dopamine in someone by telling him or her a compliment after meeting.

A simple one is fine. "You looked really nice tonight" is good for someone whom you might want to date. "You performed so well" can spark a friendship. Make someone feel important, validated, and better about their insecurities, and you have hit the jackpot for future contact.

You don't want to make rude compliments. "You looked good despite your weight" is an example of something that might get you slapped. Find a compliment that is not offensive. Also, mean it. People can sense insincerity and an insincere compliment can really put someone off.

Chapter 6: Problems With Making Friends

You may feel discouraged that everyone seems to have friends but you. For some reason, your life or your personality just does not seem to be conducive to friendships. You feel lonely and isolated as you struggle to figure out why no one likes you and why you can't get out there and make friends. As humans are social creatures, this can be the worst feeling in the world.

The truth is that you are not alone. Many people face problems making friends. The difference between you and those other people is that you are doing something about it by reading this book. You can learn to navigate the common problems barring you from making friends and find solutions.

When Your Life Circumstances Interfere With Your Social Life

Various life circumstances can stop you from making friends. It's hard to make friends when you are always at work, you are isolated geographically, or you don't have money to go out. It can also be hard when you are in a new location or suffer from a disability or handicap that makes going out hard. If your significant other is jealous and prevents you from making friends, you are in a bad spot because you are enduring a type of abuse. Some people are psychologically barred from making friends, either because of severe social anxiety, PTSD, or other issues. A speech impediment can make it hard for you to talk to others because no one can understand you.

Navigating Disabilities

If you have some type of disability, you may find support groups or activities for people with like disabilities. There are activities like wheelchair basketball or autism support groups, for instance.

Often, you can go out and have just as much fun with a disability as others. It is only in your head if you think that you can't socialize or that people won't like you if you're disabled. Take your medications, use a walker or crutches or a wheelchair, and be yourself.

Speech therapy is ideal if you have a speech impediment or some other communication issue. Learn to read lips if you are deaf.

Some people who have been through trauma can't socialize out of fear. Soldiers with PTSD are a common example. You should attend regular therapy to learn how to cope with anxiety while in social situations. You should not let a mental disability or psychological one keep you isolated and trapped in the house.

The Internet can be a great asset for those with disabilities. You can find friends from the comfort of your home. You can also find support groups and chat rooms for people who suffer the same issues that you do. But don't let your disability make you think that you are not a viable friend. You can still go out and find plenty of people willing to be your friend.

Finding Time And Money

If you barely have time to eat and sleep on top of work, you won't have time to make friends. The best way around this is to set aside some time when you sacrifice sleep for socializing.

Often, people say they don't' have time after work, but the reality is that they just go home from work and collapse before the TV. They don't make time. If you make time, you will find it in your busy schedule. Put a big priority number one before socializing to make it part of your schedule.

Another key is to forget needing money to socialize. You don't need to be rich to get out. There are plenty of free or cheap activities out there. Even if you go to a bar, you can get a cheap drink or water and sip on that as you socialize. There is no need to have money to go out.

Geographic Issues

If you live somewhere that is isolated, your best friend can be the Internet. You can find friends online and travel to meet them or invite them to visit you.

It may also be time to move. If your area is so isolated that you are unhappy, you should not endure it any longer. Being isolated can lead to depression [22]. People need human relationships and connections to feel happy.

Some areas may allow you to make friends, but there is not much to do. This is a common problem in small towns. It can be hard to make new friends when you know everyone and there is nothing local to do to make new friends. The solution is to either move, invent something to do with your friends, or visit activities and social centers in nearby towns.

When People Don't Seem Interested In Starting Friendships With You

A common problem people face when they start socializing is the sense that no one wants to start friendships. It is common to blame yourself and to think you are doing something wrong. You may be, but the issue may also be the people you are socializing with.

First, you must consider that maybe you are trying to enter the wrong group. Perhaps you have nothing in common with these people, so they are not interested in getting to know you. Perhaps they have all known each other since kindergarten and are too close-minded to allow a new friend. You can find a "Freeze effect" in some communities, where people are not interested in outsiders challenging their set routines and beliefs. By adulthood, you should have realized the universal truth that not everyone is friendly and nice.

In some communities, such as large cities, people have learned to be protective of themselves. If you are nice and chatting someone up on the subway, that person may assume you are trying to steal her purse. You can encounter a lot of unfriendliness in big cities, which is born out of a need to keep safe. Therefore, you should focus on meeting people through activities, where you look less suspicious than if you are talking to strangers in public places.

Second, consider that maybe your approach is wrong. If you appear too cold, shy, or submissive, you can make people feel uncomfortable because they are seeking confidence and assertiveness. If you don't smile enough, you may seem unfriendly. If you barely speak and don't volunteer any information about yourself, you end conversations before they can start and give people the sense that they can't get to know you.

You can't just greet people or say nothing at all and expect people to come to you. You must inject yourself into their worlds by drawing attention to yourself and going up to them. A greeting is not enough. You must actually try to make conversation.

You must ask people about themselves and show interest. If that doesn't seem to work, share something interesting or amusing about yourself. Remember, you must be an ambi-conversationalist, asking questions *and* disclosing bits about yourself.

Sometimes, the burden of inviting people out falls on you. You can chat all day and night, but the person still won't reach out. You must initiate the idea of going out. "Here's my number. Text me and I'll let you know when the next fishing derby is." That's an example of how you can find someone's interests and then act on it to hang out.

You may expect a friendship to bloom after one conversation. Or you jump in too quickly, inviting someone out after one meeting. The other person is still skeptical as he or she gets to know you. It is far better to extend an invitation, or expect one, after a few interactions, so that the mere exposure effect has set in. Remember, it takes a few exposures for people to feel sure about you.

Give it time and don't get discouraged after one setback. Perhaps someone rejected you or doesn't seem interested. That doesn't mean that you have failed altogether. Don't overgeneralize the situation and feel that you have failed in making friends. Just keep trying, with that person and with others.

Maybe people have invited you out and you've said no. Now they have given up. You can fix that by apologizing and inviting them out now. Prove that you want to go out. Don't be flaky and expect people to keep trying.

You may also not make plans that fit the other person's interests or schedule. Ask some questions to find out what and when is best. Be sensitive to the other person. Making friends in adulthood often requires some careful negotiation, since everyone has work, school, kids, and other commitments. Don't give up. After a while, your schedules will magically work together on night and you get to hang out and take your friendship to the next stage. In the meantime, you can chat and get to know each other digitally through social media or texting.

When You Don't Have Friends At All

Earlier in this book, you learned that having a friend can help you make other friends through social proof [9]. Obviously, this advice does more harm than good if you have no friends at all. How can you possibly get started?

Luckily for you, you don't have to have friends to make friends. You can strike out on your own and do well making new friends. The first key is to attend meetings or activities that interest you to put yourself out there. The second key is to actually talk to people, instead of expecting them to come to you. Seldom will people come to you, but they will appreciate it if you go up to them and try to strike up a conversation using the tips outlined in this book.

Quality Over Quantity

Truly popular people with billions of friends may be great people, but no one can have profoundly deep friendships with so many people. At least ninety percent of those friendships are likely to be surface ones with no depth. Therefore, don't feel bad if you don't have a huge friend group. One really good, loyal friend beats fifty thousand friends you barely know or care about.

Value quality over quantity. Get to know someone and be discerning. Only entertain the friends who make you feel good, who seem to actually like you, and who don't throw up red flags of danger.

Conclusion

Being able to walk up to a person, introduce yourself, and dive right into a conversation may be an art that has eluded you thus far. But with the science-based tips in this book, you should be more than ready to enter the realm of social confidence and comfort.

Being social does not mean that you have to alter your personality to become extroverted. You just have to start doing more extroverted things at times. That includes starting conversations and not being a wallflower at parties. Actually lead meetings and bring up ideas. Talk to people and ask them questions.

Talking to people is easy. You just have to find topics you both like talking about. Observing a person or asking them questions can help you find these topics. The sweet spot is the topic that makes a conversation go on for hours, without either of you getting bored.

It is also important to observe someone's conversational style. Use their sensory modal system and an assertive way of speaking when replying to people. This shows that you are confident, while avoiding misunderstandings.

Most people like confidence. Wearing red, having confident body language, maintaining eye contact, and speaking first are all ways to show your confidence. People will feel more comfortable around you and you will get more conversation and more friends as a result.

You should also use the advice of Dr. Robert Cialdini and Dale Carnegie. These wise men wrote great books about how to appeal to people. Using their knowledge can help you unlock many great friendships.

To make friends, you must leave your shell. You must get out and talk to people in new situations. Trying new activities or saying yes to invitations are good ways to get out there. Even if you have moved to a new city, it's more than possible to use the Internet to find new activities and friends, and even dates.

With something as great as conversation in your back pocket, you will find that life treats you better. As people like you, they will extend job opportunities, favors, and introductions to new friends. You can enter entirely new circles of people just by impressing one person. Be yourself and speak well, and you will make plenty of friends.

Making friends as an adult is not easy, or so people say. You can prove them wrong now. You have everything you need to start making friends and having great, even substantial, conversations. You just have to practice and put what you have learned here into action.

Stop being a wallflower. Actually walk into the center of the room and make yourself heard. People will come to you if you know how to talk and present yourself as a confident person. As you practice, you will get better and start to make more friends. With more friends, you will make yet more.

References

1 Daniel Campbell-Meiklejohn, Arndis Simonsen, Chris D. Frith and Nathaniel D. Daw. *Independent Neural Computation of Value from Other People's Confidence*. Journal of Neuroscience 18 January 2017, 37 (3) 673-684; DOI: https://doi.org/10.1523/JNEUROSCI.4490-15.2016

2 Longo, Michael. *Distortions of Perceived Volume and Length of Body*. ResearchGate. Cortex 111:74-86 DOI: 10.1016/j.cortex.2018.10.016.

3 Dr. Lawrence Michael Cameron. *Stinking Thinking: Think to Live Well Again. Taking on Maladaptive Cognitions and Dealing with Cognitive Distortions*. CreateSpace Independent Publishing Platform. ISBN-13: 978-1491047231.

4 Carolyn Parkinson, Adam M. Kleinbaum, & Thalia Wheatley. *Similar neural responses predict*

friendship. Journal of Nature Communications, Vol 9, Article # 332. 2018.

5   Facts and Statistics. (2019). *Anxiety and Depression Association of America.* https://adaa.org/about-adaa/press-room/facts-statistics

6   Gardner, B., Sheals, K., & McGowan, L. (2014). Putting habit into practice, and practice into habit: a process evaluation and exploration of the acceptability of a habit-based dietary behavior change intervention. Int J Behav Nutr Phys Act. 2014; 11: 135. doi: 10.1186/s12966-014-0135-7.

7   Carney, DR., Cuddy, A., & Yap, A. (2010). *Power Posing: Brief Nonverbal Displays Affect Neuroendocrine Levels and Risk Tolerance.* Psychological Science, Vol 1-6, DOI: 10.1177/0956797610383437

8   Renee Baron. *What Type Am I?* 1998. Penguin Books. ISBN-13: 978-0140269413

9   Cialdini, R. (2008). *Influence: The Psychology of Persuasion, 5th Ed.* Allyn and Bacon. ISBN-13: 9 78-0061241895

10 Yoshimoto, S. et al. (2014). *Pupil Response and the Subliminal Mere Exposure Effect.* PLOS One. 9(2): e90670. doi: 10.1371/journal.pone.0090670

11 Yaffe, Philip. *The 7% Rule: Fact, Fiction, or Misunderstanding.* Ubiquity. Volume 2011, Number October (2011), Pages 1-5. DOI: 10.1145/2043155.2043156.

12 O'Doherty, J., et al. *Beauty of a Smile: The Role of the Medial Orbitofrontal Cortex in Facial Attractiveness.* Neuropsychologica. 2003. Vol. 41, pp. 147-155. https://pure.mpg.de/rest/items

/item_2614428/component/file_2623264/conte
nt

13 Bandler, R., Roberti, A., & Fitzpatrick, O. (2013). *The Ultimate Introduction to NLP: How to Build A Successful Life.* HarperCollins. ISBN: 978-0007497416.

14 Carmody, Dennis & Lewis, Michael. *Brain Activation When Hearing One's Own and Others' Names.* Brain Res. 2006 Oct 20; 1116(1): 153–158.

15 Published online 2006 Sep 7. doi: 10.1016/j.brainres.2006.07.121

16 Lindquist, Kristen, et al. *The Brain Basis of Positive and Negative Affect: Evidence from a Meta-Analysis of the Human Neuroimaging Literature.* Cereb Cortex. 2016 May; 26(5): 1910–

1922. Published online 2015 Jan 28. doi: 10.1093/cercor/bhv001

17 Carnegie, Dale. *How to Win Friends and Influence People.* Pocket Books. 1998. ISBN-13: 978-0671027032.

18 Elliot, A. J., Tracy, J. L., Pazda, A. D., & Beall, A. T. (in press). *Red enhances women's attractiveness to men: First evidence suggesting universality.* Journal of Experimental Social Psychology.

19 Carr, E. & Winkielman, P. (2014). *When Mirroring is both Simple and Smart: How Mimicry can be Embodied, Adaptive, and Non-Representational.* Frontiers of Human Neuroscience. 8: 505.

20 Weger, Harry, et al. *The Relative Effectiveness of in Initial Interactions.* International Journal of

Listening. Vol 28. Issue 1, https://doi.org/10.1080/10904018.2013.813234.

21 Newton, Claire. *The Five Conversation Skills.* Web. N.d. http://www.clairenewton.co.za/my-articles/the-five-communication-styles.html.

22 Moreland, Richard & Beach, Scott. *Exposure Effects in the Classroom: The Development of Affinity Among Students.* 1992. JOURNAL OF EXPERIMENTAL SOCIAL PSYCHOLOGY, 28(3), 255-276. http://dx.doi.org/10.1016/0022-1031(92)90055-O

23 Matthews, T. et al. *Social Isolation, Loneliness, and Depression in Young Adulthood: A Behavioral Genetic Analysis.* Social Psychiatry & Psychiatric Epidemiology. 2016. Vol 51, pp. 339-348. doi: 10.1007/s00127-016-1178-7.

Disclaimer

The information contained in this book and its components, is meant to serve as a comprehensive collection of strategies that the author of this book has done research about. Summaries, strategies, tips and tricks are only recommendations by the author, and reading this book will not guarantee that one's results will exactly mirror the author's results.

The author of this book has made all reasonable efforts to provide current and accurate information for the readers of this book. The author and its associates will not be held liable for any unintentional errors or omissions that may be found.

The material in the book may include information by third parties. Third party materials comprise of opinions expressed by their owners. As such, the author of this book does not assume responsibility or liability for any third party material or opinions.

The publication of third party material does not constitute the author's guarantee of any information, products, services, or opinions contained within third party material. Use of third party material does not guarantee that your results will mirror our results. Publication of such third party material is simply a recommendation and expression of the author's own opinion of that material.

Whether because of the progression of the Internet, or the unforeseen changes in company policy and editorial submission guidelines, what is stated as fact at the time of this writing may become outdated or inapplicable later.

This book is copyright ©2019 by **John Guzman** with all rights reserved. It is illegal to redistribute, copy, or create derivative works from this book whole or in parts. No parts of this report may be reproduced or retransmitted in any forms whatsoever without the written expressed and signed permission from the author.

Lightning Source UK Ltd.
Milton Keynes UK
UKHW010138070621
385039UK00001BC/39